# THE PASSION SUFFERED BY THE HEART OF JESUS

*Prayerful Reflections on the Stations of the Cross*

LAURA MARIE DURANT, OCDS

The Passion Suffered by the Heart of Jesus
Prayerful Reflections on the Stations of the Cross

Author photo by Holland America Line

ISBN 978-1-7330439-0-8

*To my dearest Lucy and Kathy. You have both brought me closer to Him through your complete surrender to His holy will. May you both rest in the Heart of Jesus eternally.*

# Contents

# INTRODUCTION

When I first began to respond to the call to write reflections on the way of the cross, I did not know where Jesus was leading me. However, His firm but gentle tug was not something I could resist for long. When a loved one persistently calls to your heart, how can you not respond, especially when the loved one is the Son of God?

After reflecting on the stations and writing these reflections, I believe Jesus gives us His greatest teaching in His Passion. Through His ultimate sacrifice, He provides the answers to all our struggles, trials, and questions. He showed us how we are to live in this life so we can live forever with Him in the next.

These reflections were written by surrendering myself to the Heart of Jesus. It was while resting there that I was filled with His compassion, love, and yearning to be united to all mankind.

While these stations can be used as reflections during Lent, or leading up to and on the feast of the Sacred Heart of Jesus, I believe Jesus desires our reflection on His Passion to be continuous. So I urge you to reflect on His Passion regularly, especially in times of difficulty, trials, and suffering. I trust in doing so you will find, as I have, a great source of comfort, consolation, and healing.

# How to Use This Book

As a person goes through a difficult experience, what we see on the outside is never as revealing as knowing what is happening in that person's heart. This book is comprised of prayers and reflections that allow you to experience what the Heart of Jesus experienced as He lived His Passion. These prayerful reflections, I pray, will allow you to see the love with which Jesus lived out His way of the cross, and how, in doing so, He gave us many gifts and lessons on how to live and love in our own trials and suffering.

## INITIAL PRAYER

The book begins with a prayer that stirs a desire to console the Heart of Jesus for the pain He suffered in His Passion and asks for the grace to live as He did. You may also find this prayer useful as a preparation prayer for the Lenten season.

## MAIN SECTION

The main section of this book leads you through the way of the cross using the Scriptural Stations proposed by Saint John Paul II. The Scriptural Stations are slightly different from the traditional Stations of the Cross. (The traditional Stations of the Cross are generally celebrated in services on Friday during Lent and are the stations that are found on the walls and stained-glass windows of Catholic churches.) The Scriptural Stations of the Cross were first celebrated by Pope John Paul II on Good Friday in 1991. They are meant to be used as an alternative to the traditional Stations of the Cross, and they allow one to reflect more deeply on the scriptural accounts of the Passion. You can find more on the history of the Stations of the Cross on the Vatican website.[1]

Within the main section of this book, each chapter starts with a scripture passage related to that particular station in the Passion.

The Bible passage is followed by a Reflection Prayer and a Closing Prayer. Both prayers are written from the heart, my heart, while meditating and resting in the Heart of Jesus and coming to understand, as one would of a dear loved one, what occurred in the depths of His Heart during His Passion. At first glance, both prayers might seem to be one and the same. However, there is a slight difference between the two.

The Reflection Prayer is more of a reflection of my own reaction, as well as the state of His Heart, during the events in the Bible passage. The Closing Prayer is more of a plea to Jesus as I desire transformation of my own heart and ask for His help in consoling His Heart for the pain He suffered.

You may find it helpful to have your Bible handy to reference the passage in each chapter. You may like to read

---

1 Vatican. Office for the Liturgical Celebrations of the Supreme Pontiff. "The Way of the Cross," Accessed February 7, 2019. http://www.vatican.va/news_services/liturgy/documents/ns_lit_doc_via-crucis_en.html.

more of the passage that surrounds it, as well as journal to write down any thoughts or feelings you may have while reflecting on each Bible passage.

## FINAL PRAYER

The book closes with a prayer that is a summary of the prayerful reflections throughout the book. You may want to say it daily to reflect on His Passion, especially during Lent and on the feast of the Sacred Heart of Jesus.

May you come to know His cross of love, mercy, and healing in a deeper way through these reflections. I pray these reflections bring healing to wounded hearts, soften hardened hearts and give us strength by which we can endure all the crosses we are blessed with in our own lives.

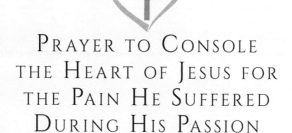

# Prayer to Console the Heart of Jesus for the Pain He Suffered During His Passion

*Jesus, help me to surrender myself always to Your will as You surrendered Yourself to Your Father.*

*Give me the faith to know that if God wishes to deliver me from suffering, He will do so.*

*Give me the wisdom to always speak the truth, but never more than what is necessary.*

*Give me the courage to endure all suffering, hardships, condemnation, and accusation as You did.*

*May all the suffering and hardships I endure be offered up for those who suffer unjustly, are tortured, forgotten, and abandoned.*

*May my only desire be to do Your will in all things and follow Your example in how we are to endure our suffering lovingly and willingly.*

*May my every waking moment be spent seeking to console Your Heart, which was pained by the rejection and neglect of so many on Your walk to Your final act of pure love.*

*May Your Heart, which was filled with so much love for us, yet also such great sorrow at the time of Your condemnation, scourging, and crucifixion, have mercy on us!*

*I beg of You, Jesus, with however much I can console Your Heart with my own imperfect love, that the mercy that pours forth from Your Heart flows onto those who do not know You, who reject You, who are lukewarm in their love for You, and who are deceived by the lies of the evil one!*

*I surrender my heart and soul into the pure and Immaculate Heart of Your blessed mother, Mary, and pray she shows me what it means to surrender all to You and unite myself to You on the cross and in Your suffering, as she did so lovingly and perfectly.*

*Jesus, my Lord, my Savior, my God, I surrender myself into Your Heart, which is my refuge, my eternal resting place.*

Then Jesus came with them to a place called Gethsemane, and he said to his disciples, "Sit here while I go over there and pray." He took along Peter and the two sons of Zebedee, and began to feel sorrow and distress. Then he said to them, "My soul is sorrowful even to death. Remain here and keep watch with me." He advanced a little and fell prostrate in prayer, saying, "My Father, if it is possible, let this cup pass from me; yet, not as I will, but as you will." When he returned to his disciples he found them asleep. He said to Peter, "So you could not keep watch with me for one hour? Watch and pray that you may not undergo the test. The spirit is willing, but the flesh is weak."

(MATTHEW 26:36–41)

# JESUS IN THE GARDEN OF GETHSEMANE

## REFLECTION PRAYER

Jesus, as You knelt before Your Father in the garden, I know Your Heart was filled with agony and pain. You knew what was to come and the excruciating pain You must suffer. But more than that, Your Heart suffered the agony of knowing Your children, who You loved so much would reject You, condemn You, torture You, and crucify You. You had given Your whole life to show them the way of love, the way of healing, the way of mercy, and now, You would show them the way of the cross.

The pain Your Heart suffered was also knowing that even after the victory You would have over death, You would still be rejected, even in this very day, this very hour, by so many of Your children! You wait, lonely day and night, waiting to be adored by Your children, waiting for them to come to visit You. You foresaw it all then.

Jesus, may my heart burn with love for You so that when I am able, I will always seek to visit You in Your tabernacle of love where You are present and ready to receive even the greatest of sinners. May my heart burn as Yours did that day in the garden of Gethsemane, so I may desire to love others so much that I am willing to endure suffering, pain, and hardship for their sake, so they may come to spend eternal life with You. May I surrender to Your will as You surrendered Yourself to the Father.

## CLOSING PRAYER

Jesus, help me surrender myself always to Your will, as You surrendered Yourself to Your Father.

Give me the faith to know that if God wishes to deliver me from suffering, He will do so.

Give me the courage to see suffering as a blessing, and to suffer it willingly as You did, so it may be a gift I can return to You, Jesus, to console Your agonizing Heart, so You may have mercy on me and all sinners throughout the world.

Then, while he was still speaking, Judas, one of the Twelve, arrived, accompanied by a crowd with swords and clubs, who had come from the chief priests, the scribes, and the elders. His betrayer had arranged a signal with them, saying, "The man I shall kiss is the one; arrest him and lead him away securely." He came and immediately went over to him and said, "Rabbi." And he kissed him. At this they laid hands on him and arrested him.

(MARK 14:43–46)

# JESUS, BETRAYED BY JUDAS, IS ARRESTED

## REFLECTION PRAYER

Jesus, how Your Heart must have been breaking, as You knew You would be betrayed by one who You loved. Yet You knew the will of Your Father and accepted it without question. When You were approached, Your courage and faith were steadfast; You did not run and hide, You remained calm. Though You were not a threat in any way, they came to You with weapons, as if they were needed to arrest You. You rightly pointed out that You had been among them so many days teaching of love, mercy, and healing, and yet today they came for You as if You would hurt them.

How Your Heart must have been saddened at that very moment. To be betrayed by one who You had loved. And the betrayal was done in a way typical of affection for one who loves another. By a kiss. How Your Heart must have been torn in two at that moment!

And then, to be arrested by those who You came to save! Who You came to show the way to life everlasting! They came at You with clubs; You responded with peaceful surrender. You knew this must come to pass for You to save us. As You looked out onto the crowd and upon the one who betrayed You, You knew this would not be the last time false accusations would be made against You or the last time You would be betrayed by those who claim to love You. Your Heart must have ached knowing this. With great love, instead of seeking revenge, You surrendered Yourself into their hands to fulfill Your Father's will.

## CLOSING PRAYER

Oh Jesus, how can I console Your Heart? Show me how I can make reparations for this injustice done to You!

*How can I ease the pain of Your Heart so full of love for mankind You would willingly allow Yourself to be betrayed, arrested and crucified by those You came to save?*

When day came the council of elders of the people met, both chief priests and scribes, and they brought him before their Sanhedrin. They said, "If you are the Messiah, tell us," but he replied to them, "If I tell you, you will not believe, and if I question, you will not respond. But from this time on the Son of Man will be seated at the right hand of the power of God." They all asked, "Are you then the Son of God?" He replied to them, "You say that I am." Then they said, "What further need have we for testimony? We have heard it from his own mouth."

(Luke 22:66–71)

# JESUS IS CONDEMNED BY THE SANHEDRIN

## REFLECTION PRAYER

Quietly You remained, and one after another spoke up to accuse You, making false allegations against You. You remained quiet. The ones who You came to save fought so hard to incriminate you! How Your Heart ached at this truth! How You desired they see You for who You are!

And then, when they questioned Your true nature, the Son of God, You spoke the truth. They could not accept it. They could not see the man who was in front of them was their Savior, their Almighty God. You knew each and every one of their hearts, their souls. You knew their aches, their pains, their wounds, their hearts. My dear Jesus, if only they knew Your love for them. If only they knew You willingly put Yourself in that very place, at that very moment, to save them. And yet, You were calm, and accepted their abuse, their violence against You.

Sadly, what happened then still happens today, my dearest Lord. There are many who make false allegations against You and Your Church! Your Heart knew it would happen then. How much pain You must have been in from knowing this!

Lord, how I wish those who do not know You, and what You've done for them, could come to know You at this very moment! How we forget the sacrifice You made for us! Forgive me, Lord, for my neglect and ingratitude. Forgive us all for the ingratitude shown to You each day when we do not acknowledge You for who You truly are—our Lord, our God, our Redeemer, our Savior. Have mercy on us, Jesus, and do not abandon us to our misery!

## CLOSING PRAYER

Forgive me, Jesus, for the ingratitude I have shown You throughout my life. Show me how I can transform my heart, so all I do is done to console Your Heart from the sadness and pain those with hardened hearts inflict upon You. Sacred Heart of Jesus, have mercy on me and on the whole world!

N ow Peter was sitting outside in the courtyard. One of the maids came over to him and said, "You too were with Jesus the Galilean." But he denied it in front of everyone, saying, "I do not know what you are talking about!" As he went out to the gate, another girl saw him and said to those who were there, "This man was with Jesus the Nazorean." Again he denied it with an oath, "I do not know the man!" A little later the bystanders came over and said to Peter, "Surely you too are one of them; even your speech gives you away." At that he began to curse and to swear, "I do not know the man." And immediately a cock crowed. Then Peter remembered the word that Jesus had spoken: "Before the cock crows you will deny me three times." He went out and began to weep bitterly.

(Matthew 26:69–75)

# JESUS IS DENIED BY PETER

## REFLECTION PRAYER

Jesus, You knew Peter's heart deeply and had great love for him. You also knew he would deny You. Although he said he would never do such a thing, Your Heart knew differently. When the time came, and Peter denied You as You had foretold, You knew the pain this would cause him. You felt it deeply in Your Heart. You knew he would suffer from knowing he had denied the One who was his Savior, the Son of God. It was his fear that kept him from acknowledging he knew You. The sadness that must have filled Your Heart when it happened, knowing the pain that filled the heart of Your beloved disciple! Yet, You had plans for him greater than he could imagine. Your love for him would consume his pain. Your Heart would heal the wounds of his heart. He would proclaim Your name, Your goodness, Your truth. You would transform him. Your Heart of mercy would redeem him and all of us!

Your Heart redeems me as well, Jesus, and all who deny You out of fear, even though we know You to be our Savior. When we cower in fear, Your Heart aches for us, too. You desire for us to be free to love You and acknowledge You as who You truly are and proclaim this truth to whoever asks if we are one of Your followers. Your Heart aches when we do not follow through and acknowledge this truth, for You know the pain we will endure when we come to realize how we have denied the truth and the One who created us, loved us, and sacrificed all for us. However, just as You did with Peter, You will redeem us, save us, and heal us if we only turn back to You.

# CLOSING PRAYER

*J esus, heal my brokenness, my wounds, the crevices in my heart that are filled with fear and pain. Permeate those areas of my heart with the love and mercy of Your Most Sacred Heart, so I may always proclaim the truth of who You are with joy—my Savior, my Redeemer, my God!*

As soon as morning came, the chief priests with the elders and scribes, that is, the whole Sanhedrin, held a council. They bound Jesus, led him away, and handed him over to Pilate. Pilate questioned him, "Are you the king of the Jews?" He said to him in reply, "You say so." The chief priests accused him of many things. Again Pilate questioned him, "Have you no answer? See how many things they accuse you of." Jesus gave him no further answer, so that Pilate was amazed.

(Mark 15:1-5)

# JESUS IS JUDGED BY PILATE

## REFLECTION PRAYER

How wretched was the jealousy in the hearts of the chief priests and elders! How You wished instead they could see You for who You truly are—their Savior, the Son of God. The hatred inflamed in the hearts of the people who were influenced by the chief priests and elders only served to pain Your Heart all the more. As both man and God, You felt rejection, abandonment, and humiliation, but also pain of seeing God's children so filled with hatred and jealously. How intense was the fear in Pilate's heart, as he could not withstand the intensity of hatred in the crowd! You said to Pilate, "My kingdom does not belong to this world. If my kingdom did belong to this world, my attendants [would] be fighting to keep me from being handed over to the Jews. But as it is, my kingdom is not here." (John 18:36)

I know Your Heart ached for Your people to see You for who You truly are, and for them to not to reject their King who, even in their sinfulness, loved them so much! How it now aches as we also reject You when we do not visit You, even as You are so available to us in so many chapels, ready and willing to comfort us, console us, and heal our sorrows. Even then You must have known how we would reject You this very day. Yet You submitted Yourself to the system of the day in order to conquer death so we may all have a chance to have eternal life.

You showed us, before Pilate and those who wished to crucify You, that fear of death is unnecessary; for what is to come after suffering and our final breath is what our heart should beat for—which is our eternal abode, our everlasting home with You, the Father, and the Holy Spirit. Whatever comes, whether accusation, condemnation, suffering—whatever we are subjected to—will never compare to the eternal bliss of our heavenly home and the joy of resting in Your arms and Heart for eternity.

## CLOSING PRAYER

Jesus, though you were accused and condemned, you remained calm and steadfast. You were innocent but condemned to die. Give me the courage to endure all suffering, hardship, and condemnation as You did.

Then Pilate took Jesus and had him scourged. And the soldiers wove a crown out of thorns and placed it on his head, and clothed him in a purple cloak, and they came to him and said, "Hail, King of the Jews!" And they struck him repeatedly.

(John 19:1–3)

SIXTH STATION

# Scourged and Crowned with Thorns, Jesus Sees the Hearts of His Abusers

## Reflection Prayer

Jesus, You were taken off by the soldiers to be scourged and then received a crown of thorns as they beat You and mocked You; they kneeled before You as their King, laughing at You. Such injustice! But You did not fight back. Instead, the tears You shed were tears of pain—not just physical pain, but the pain of knowing the hearts of those who were torturing You. You could see through their unjust and brutal behavior straight to their hearts. You could see their wounded hearts and their suffering. You could see the hearts of the bystanders who kept quiet,

31

who knew who You were but did not speak up because of fear. The bystanders could only see the hatred and evil in the eyes of the soldiers who mocked You and beat You, but You saw their hearts. You knew what You were enduring was not just for those who knew who You were, who proclaimed You the Son of God; You were enduring this for the soldiers, the chief priests, and all those in the crowd who mocked You. Your Heart had love even for them, and You knew it would take the greatest sacrifice in all of history to provide a way for even those who tortured You, denied You, and rejected You to be able, through repentance and surrendering themselves to Your mercy, to one day be healed and rest in Your Heart of mercy. You endured suffering so the most wretched of all of us could enter the kingdom of heaven if only we would turn to You for mercy and acknowledge You as Creator and Redeemer.

How we should learn from Your love, Your sacrifice, Your forgiveness! How we condemn others for the slightest misdeeds! And for those who commit atrocities, we feel justified in saying their souls are lost forever. Yet You showed us in Your great act of pure love that we are to forgive, to surrender all to You and abandon ourselves and all those who sin into Your just and merciful hands.

For what if You had given up on sinners? None of us would have a chance. Yet You were willing to be tortured and die for even the greatest of sinners. You love us all that much. Help us, Jesus, to not condemn others; help us to pray for them, especially those who hurt us. Help us no matter how hard and how difficult it is! Give us the grace to love with Your Heart, to receive Your mercy, and in turn, show others the same mercy that comes from Your Most Sacred Heart.

## CLOSING PRAYER

Jesus, You were tortured and beaten by the soldiers, yet You did not fight back because You saw their wounds. May all my suffering and hardships be offered up for all. May my only desire be to love with the love that comes from Your Heart, so I may see others as You do. Give me the grace to pray for those who wound others, that their own wounds be healed and they may reach eternal salvation.

When the chief priests and the guards saw him they cried out, "Crucify him, crucify him!" Pilate said to them, "Take him yourselves and crucify him. I find no guilt in him." ... They cried out, "Take him away, take him away! Crucify him!" Pilate said to them, "Shall I crucify your king?" The chief priests answered, "We have no king but Caesar." Then he handed him over to them to be crucified. So they took Jesus, and carrying the cross himself he went out to what is called the Place of the Skull, in Hebrew, Golgotha.

(John 19:6,15–17)

# JESUS BEARS THE CROSS AND THE PAIN OF OUR SINS

## REFLECTION PRAYER

The weight of all the sins of the world pressed upon You as they handed You the cross. The pain that pierced Your Heart was searing. The sins committed and to be committed weighed upon Your Heart. The humiliations You suffered from the mocking of the crowd and the pain from the heavy weight of the cross upon Your body was only overshadowed by the pain burning in Your Heart. You knew You would need help along the way. You were God, but also man.

You took the cross and looked up as You knew Your time on earth was almost through. While the physical pain was intense, You also knew there would soon be joy as You would be with Your Heavenly Father again, and what You came to accomplish on earth would be fulfilled.

You would provide a way for all God's children to be reconciled to God the Father through You. Generations to come would be able to be saved, and one day, after their time on earth was complete, they would spend eternity with You, the Father, and the Holy Spirit. Your Heart was filled with love knowing You would be able to give us that same love. The love from the Father would sustain You throughout the rest of Your Passion. It is the same love You give us as we carry our crosses on this earth today.

# Closing Prayer

Jesus, the pain of the cross that weighed upon You was intense, but not as intense as the pain of the sins that weighed upon Your Heart throughout Your Passion. May God have mercy on me for all the pain I caused You by my sins. May I seek to console Your Heart for all the pain my sins and the sins of the whole world have caused You. I thank You for the love with which You carried the cross, and the love with which, in Your great mercy, You give me to strengthen me as I carry my cross today.

They pressed into service a passer-by, Simon, a Cyrenian, who was coming in from the country, the father of Alexander and Rufus, to carry his cross.

(Mark 15:21)

# Jesus is Helped by Simon the Cyrenian to Carry the Cross

## Reflection Prayer

Like many crosses we experience in life, this cross was too much to bear on Your own. While You were God and man, You allowed Yourself to feel the full weight of the cross, to be overwhelmed by it, to experience what we experience with our crosses. So because of Your experience of this, we all know we can turn to You as someone who completely understands when our crosses are too much to bear on our own.

To show us how we are to allow others to help us, You accepted the help of Simon. You could have rejected help and said, "No, I am to carry this alone," but instead You humbled Yourself, allowing Yourself to be seen as too weak to carry the cross alone. You also desired to transform another heart as You made Your way during Your final hours here on earth.

Simon, whose heart You knew, would be greatly blessed by helping the Savior of the world in His final hours. Simon did not know how his life would be changed that day or the important role he would play in all of human history, but You knew. It pleased You to bless him in this way. He was forced into this role, as we are during the many times we do not necessarily desire to help others carry their crosses, but we do it out of duty. No doubt he came to realize who You were. If we are graced with hearts opened at the ability to help others, we see the amazing blessings we have in helping them with their cross and how blessed we are to do so, just as Simon must have come to realize with all the pain and suffering You were experiencing for our sake. Your focus turned once more to this man, who knew not who You were, who was reluctant to help, and no doubt had other plans of his own that day. Instead, You had Your own plans for him, to give him the blessing of assisting the Savior of the world on

His final walk on this earth. How it pleased Your Heart to continue to help another one of God's children while You were still able to in the flesh.

## CLOSING PRAYER

*Jesus, help me to see all of my crosses, and the ability to help others with theirs, as the true blessing they are. Let me see myself as blessed as Simon was when he was chosen to help You with Your cross. Help me to experience the joy in Your Heart and the humility that comes when my own cross is physically or mentally too much to bear and I need to allow others to help me. May I also turn to You and surrender to You the suffering I experience from my crosses. May I see this suffering as the blessing and grace it is. May I surrender all to You so you can use me as Your vessel to bring glory to Your name.*

A large crowd of people followed Jesus, including many women who mourned and lamented him. Jesus turned to them and said, "Daughters of Jerusalem, do not weep for me; weep instead for yourselves and for your children, for indeed, the days are coming when people will say, 'Blessed are the barren, the wombs that never bore and the breasts that never nursed.' At that time, people will say to the mountains, 'Fall upon us!' and to the hills, 'Cover us!' for if these things are done when the wood is green what will happen when it is dry?"

(Luke 23:27–31)

# THE HEART OF JESUS IS MOVED AS HE MEETS THE WOMEN OF JERUSALEM

## REFLECTION PRAYER

Jesus, how You were moved with compassion when You met the women weeping for You. How You wished to ease their pain. You knew that in their hearts they knew You for who You truly were. You saw them as the unique creations they were—blessed, gentle masterpieces created by God. You saw the struggles they faced as women, and the struggles all women would face throughout history to this very day.

You saw them living out their true nature, as they were created to be by God. We were created to love and to have compassion and mourn when others are in pain. While Your Heart ached for the sadness they felt in their hearts, You knew they would be an example for future generations for how our true nature is to respond to hatred, violence, and cruelty done to those who are innocent. Those blessed women were blessed indeed. They knew You, and while their hearts were in pain during those moments, the joy they experience in their eternal union with You now is without end.

## Closing Prayer

Jesus, help me to respond to those in pain with compassion and to mourn the unjust suffering of others. Help me to see hearts as You do. Help me to love with a pure heart, a compassionate heart, a merciful heart. Help me to live out my true nature as a child of God.

When they came to the place called the Skull, they crucified him and the criminals there, one on his right, the other on his left. Then Jesus said, "Father, forgive them, they know not what they do."

(Luke 23:33–34)

# JESUS IS CRUCIFIED

## REFLECTION PRAYER

What horror, what tragedy as they nailed Your hands and feet to the wood of the cross! The unspeakable pain You must have felt! The pain You endured for our sake! How my heart breaks as I imagine what You endured for my salvation! How often and easily do we forget the pain You endured for us. How easily do we get swept away in our daily lives and forget what You suffered for our sake. Jesus, may we never forget what You endured to save us and the rest of humanity.

And in Your loving way, You not only endured the pain of those who tortured You, mocked You, and crucified You, but You asked the Father to forgive them. You knew that if they truly knew who You were, they would not be doing this to You. And, if they truly knew what they were doing, they would fall to their knees and beg for mercy! Had they known they were crucifying the Savior of the world, they would have prostrated before You, surrendered themselves to You and begged for forgiveness! But alas, they nailed Your hands and feet to the wood, and mocked You, saying "He saved others, let him save himself if he is the chosen one, the Messiah of God." (Luke 23:35) In the midst of all this, You responded by asking Your Father to forgive them.

## CLOSING PRAYER

Jesus, show me how to forgive others when I am wronged. Help me to not seek revenge but to be merciful and ask for forgiveness on their behalf. Help me to endure the pain and humiliations that may come my way by surrendering all to You. Help me see this suffering as a blessing and grace that allows me to give all glory to You.

Now one of the criminals hanging there reviled Jesus, saying, "Are you not the Messiah? Save yourself and us." The other, however, rebuking him, said in reply, "Have you no fear of God, for you are subject to the same condemnation? And indeed, we have been condemned justly, for the sentence we received corresponds to our crimes, but this man has done nothing criminal." Then he said, "Jesus, remember me when you come into your kingdom." He replied to him, "Amen, I say to you, today you will be with me in Paradise."

(Luke 23:39–43)

# Jesus Promises His Kingdom to the Good Thief

## Reflection Prayer

O Jesus, how Your Heart rejoiced as the criminal acknowledged You and saw You for who You truly are. How You desired all people who were there that day know You as their savior. You loved all so much, as You suffered so much for them. The criminal, a sinner just like the rest of us, realized his sins and acknowledged he was deserving of his sentence, but You, on the other hand, were just, and undeserving of being where You were. How Your

Heart rejoiced as You would be with this sinner, who saw You for who You truly are, in Your heavenly kingdom.

What an example this criminal is for all of us, that we are to acknowledge our sinfulness and acknowledge You for who You truly are. That is Your desire—and how You and all in the heavens rejoice when a sinner repents and turns to You for mercy and forgiveness! How Your Heart never tires of showering a repentant sinner with mercy, love, and peace! Your Heart is truly an endless source of mercy.

Even on the cross, You were pleased to help one more heart be changed forever. Your desire to save all humanity, and each one of us individually, never ceased. You gave Your all each moment of every day of Your life here on Earth. Even in Your very last moments, You never stopped reaching out to save us.

## CLOSING PRAYER

Jesus, help me to never be afraid to acknowledge You as my Savior and King. Even when I sin, help me always to remember that, even on the cross, You were always eager to receive the greatest of sinners if they only turned to You and sought Your mercy and forgiveness. Jesus, may Your name be praised forever and forever, and may Your name be glorified in the heavens and on the earth for the great sacrifice You made for all mankind.

Standing by the cross of Jesus were his mother and his mother's sister, Mary the wife of Clopas, and Mary of Magdala. When Jesus saw his mother and the disciple there whom he loved, he said to his mother, "Woman, behold, your son." Then he said to the disciple, "Behold, your mother." And from that hour the disciple took her into his home.

(John 19:25–27)

# JESUS SPEAKS TO HIS MOTHER AND THE DISCIPLE

## REFLECTION PRAYER

Jesus, how Your Heart must have hurt to see Your mother in so much agony. To see her son up on the cross suffering before He would die that day. You knew she needed comfort, someone who You knew would care for her, love her. So You turned to Your beloved disciple for him to care for her after You would be on Earth no more. But more than that, as You gave her to Your beloved disciple to care for her, You also gave her the rest of humanity to care for. You knew all of God's children needed a mother so beautiful, so pure, so loving, so understanding of who You were and understanding of Your will.

She had been there with You all Your life: from the moment of Your conception to Your birth; as You took Your first steps, said Your first words; when she was in great anxiety as You were lost for three days. She watched You grow older, as Your adopted father here on earth, Joseph, cared for You and taught You his craft. She assisted You in Your ministry and observed the wonders of Your miracles and heavenly works. She knew Your Heart, as only a mother can. So of course Your mother would be the perfect mother for us all, to care for us, to love us, to pray for us, and to be an intercessor on our behalf as we seek to unite ourselves to You through her.

Her Immaculate Heart burns with love for us. She desires that all of God's children turn to You. You knew she would always lead us to You, to Your mercy and Your grace. While she suffered in agony as You hung on the cross, You knew the glory that would await her in heaven for eternity. How blessed are we, that You would share Your perfect, beautiful, and pure mother with us. Let us find consolation in her most Immaculate Heart and her nurturing warmth, which consoles the hearts of so many wounded. May we all come to You through Mary, seek her love, seek her prayers, and may she always lead us to Your Most Sacred Heart!

## CLOSING PRAYER

*Jesus, I entrust my heart and soul to your blessed mother, Mary, and pray she helps me to know what it means to surrender all to You and unite myself to Your will as she did, so purely, lovingly, and perfectly.*

It was now about noon and darkness came over the whole land until three in the afternoon because of an eclipse of the sun. Then the veil of the temple was torn down the middle. Jesus cried out in a loud voice, "Father, into your hands I commend my spirit"; and when he had said this he breathed his last.

(Luke 23:44–46)

# Jesus Dies on the Cross

## Reflection Prayer

What pain You suffered hanging there on the cross for hours with the nails driven into Your hands and feet—the piercing pain You must have endured! When they gave You wine mixed with gall to drink, You denied it, wanting not to ease the pain but to endure it willingly and lovingly. Again, You continued to teach us how to suffer and surrender all to our Heavenly Father—even the greatest of suffering.

In Your final moments, You said, "I thirst." How blessed was the person who gave You Your last drink from the sponge with wine. May we all run to You to console Your thirst for our love and surrender all to You. May we seek to always console Your Heart and quench Your thirst for all hearts and souls, and we pray that they return to You. Show us how; teach us, dear Jesus, how to turn the rest of our lives over to You in each moment of every day.

When it was time, You handed Yourself over to the Father and taught us how we should hand ourselves over as well—hand over our spirit, hand over our lives, lay our spirit into Your hands, into Your Heart, and forever rest in the peace of knowing You will never leave us or abandon us.

You lived every moment of Your life with pure love for all of mankind. You were always pointing us to the Father. Even in Your last moments, You never once stopped loving all of us—those who knew who You truly were and proclaimed You as their savior, as well as those who did not and tortured You, mocked You, and crucified You.

## CLOSING PRAYER

*J*esus, may we look to Your example in Your Passion for how we are to live every moment of our lives, in every situation, with every decision we encounter. You have given us all we will ever need, because You gave us every part of Yourself; You gave Your life. I pray for the intercession of our blessed mother, Mary, and all the saints, so that in each moment of every day, I may give You my life. I surrender myself into Your Heart, my refuge, my eternal resting place.

When it was evening, there came a rich man from Arimathea named Joseph, who was himself a disciple of Jesus. He went to Pilate and asked for the body of Jesus; then Pilate ordered it to be handed over. Taking the body, Joseph wrapped it [in] clean linen and laid it in his new tomb that he had hewn in the rock. Then he rolled a huge stone across the entrance to the tomb and departed.

(Matthew 27:57–60)

# JESUS IS PLACED IN THE TOMB

## REFLECTION PRAYER

How painful it must have been for Your mother as Your lifeless body was taken down from the cross, to hold You in the flesh one last time. Due to the kindness of a man named Joseph from Arimathea, You were wrapped in clean linens, and Your body was given its last resting place in the tomb here on earth before the fulfillment of Your resurrection to come.

The women stayed close, carefully observing where You were laid, as they prepared for when they would return to anoint Your body with oils. Sad and distraught were

Your followers, but You would soon deliver them from their sadness and bring them great joy.

May we all take the example of Joseph, who in his kindness reached out to assist in defending Your dignity with clean linens, and took it upon himself to find a proper burial place for You. May we seek to always do the right thing, to act regardless of our fear, and treat others with dignity, kindness, and compassion.

## CLOSING PRAYER

J esus, may I seek to care for others, and treat them with respect and dignity, even when it is not popular or even if it could cost me something great. Let no man, woman, or child be a stranger to me or be someone else's problem. May I see them all as You do, created in the image and likeness of God unique, beautiful, and beloved children of God.

When the sabbath was over, Mary Magdalene, Mary, the mother of James, and Salome bought spices so that they might go and anoint him. Very early when the sun had risen, on the first day of the week, they came to the tomb. They were saying to one another, "Who will roll back the stone for us from the entrance to the tomb?" When they looked up, they saw that the stone had been rolled back; it was very large. On entering the tomb they saw a young man sitting on the right side, clothed in a white robe, and they were utterly amazed. He said to them, "Do not be amazed! You seek Jesus of Nazareth, the crucified. He has been raised; he is not here. Behold, the place where they laid him. But go and tell his disciples and Peter, 'He is going before you to Galilee; there you will see him, as he told you.'"

(Mark 16:1–7)

# JESUS, HIS HEART FILLED WITH JOY, RISES FROM THE DEAD

## REFLECTION PRAYER

Praise Jesus, our Almighty Father! Our Savior has indeed saved the world and all those who love Him! He conquered death and sin and rose to new life!

Jesus, Your story is one of love—love in joy, love in suffering, love in every aspect of daily life. You lived Your life fully and died with pure love in Your Heart. What joy must You have been feeling when the women came to look for Your lifeless body to anoint You, but You had risen just as You had foretold.

Jesus, as we contemplate Your Passion, the pain You endured, and Your suffering caused by our sins and those of the whole world, we know Your Heart was filled with joy at this point, for You had fulfilled Your mission on earth and would soon give Your disciples what they needed to continue bringing hearts and souls to You. We, too, rejoice as we contemplate Your resurrection, how You defeated sin and death and rose to eternal life so that we may have eternal life too. You showed us death is not the end—it is just the beginning of eternal joy with You, the Father, and the Holy Spirit, forever, in heaven.

## CLOSING PRAYER

*J esus, may my heart sing with praise and adoration for the gift of You and Your life, Your teaching, Your example, Your healing, Your love, and Your peace that extends to the farthest reaches of the earth. May my heart shout with joy to the hearts who know You not, to the hearts that desire You but are afraid and deny You, to the hearts that know You and desire to know You even more. Lord, You showed me throughout the way of the cross how to endure suffering, how to not fear death but how to embrace it willingly, how to give all to You as You gave all of Yourself to Your Father, so I can one day be laid in my own tomb, only to then live forever with You, the Father, and the Holy Spirit in heaven for eternity.*

# CONTEMPLATE HIS PASSION DAILY

L et us take time to reflect on Jesus's Passion and death on the cross each day. Let us consider how Jesus gave His all in each moment, enduring pain and suffering so lovingly and willingly so we may live forever.

# DAILY PRAYER TO
# CONTEMPLATE THE PASSION
# OF THE HEART OF JESUS

Jesus, You never tired of showing mercy and teaching us
how we should live our lives here on earth in relationship
with You and in relationship with others.

As we await Your coming again, let us reflect on the pain You
endured, the hardships, the mocking, the accusations, the
torture, Your crucifixion and how You loved us completely
all the way through Your Passion.

You blessed others even in Your Passion as You walked Your
final walk here on earth.

*You humbled Yourself when You could not carry the cross alone, showing us how to help others with their crosses and how to allow others to help us carry ours.*

*Your Heart ached as You saw the women mourn Your suffering, and Your Heart ached for theirs.*

*Your Heart was always concerned for the other, even in Your own suffering and death.*

*You were always leading us to the Father, even in these last moments of Your life on earth. You abandoned Your will to the Father in each moment, with every ounce of strength that You had left.*

*You tirelessly took every opportunity to suffer for our sake so we may have eternal life with You.*

*Your Heart rejoiced when the criminal acknowledged You for who You were—for he would be with You in heaven. You prayed for those that tortured You, crucified You, and You showed us the way in which we should love others that hurt us.*

*Jesus, You are my Savior, You are my God, my Redeemer. You gave all for me so I could spend forever with You. May I never forget Your Passion, and help me to console Your Most Sacred Heart by surrendering all to You, as You surrendered Yourself to the Father.*

*Jesus, my Lord, my God, I am Yours. I throw myself into Your Heart of mercy and surrender my life into Your hands.*

# ABOUT THE AUTHOR

**L**aura Marie Durant writes prayers and reflections for her blog, HealingHeartofJesus.com, which are meant for anyone who struggles with anxiety and depression to any degree, as well as for those who care for them. She started her blog in response to a call to spread the message of the mercy, healing, and love found in the Sacred Heart of Jesus. She's received great healing through daily prayer before Jesus in the adoration chapel, experiencing what it means to rest in His Heart.

She is a Catholic Christian and member of the Secular Order of Discalced Carmelites of the Province of St. Therese (Oklahoma Province). Her Carmelite name is "of the Immaculate Heart of Mary." Living Carmelite spirituality has transformed her prayer life and brought her to a greater love of Mary and her most Immaculate Heart and the Sacred Heart of Jesus. She is humbled by the many blessings Our Lord has given her and her husband in order to allow them to spread His love. She prays these reflections bring anyone who reads them closer to the Sacred Heart of Jesus through Mary and her most Immaculate Heart.

She's blessed to be married to her husband, John, for more than ten years, and she is the mother of their bulldog, Winston. She received her bachelor's degree in Psychology from the University of Texas at Austin, and a master's degree in Professional Counseling from Texas State University-San Marcos.

CPSIA information can be obtained
at www.ICGtesting.com
Printed in the USA
FFHW011934061119
56000005-61842FF